Attitude

Discover The True Power Of A Positive Attitude

By Ace McCloud
Copyright © 2014

Disclaimer

The information provided in this book is designed to provide helpful information on the subjects discussed. This book is not meant to be used, nor should it be used, to diagnose or treat any medical condition. For diagnosis or treatment of any medical problem, consult your own physician. The publisher and author are not responsible for any specific health or allergy needs that may require medical supervision and are not liable for any damages or negative consequences from any treatment, action, application or preparation, to any person reading or following the information in this book. Any references included are provided for informational purposes only. Readers should be aware that any websites or links listed in this book may change.

Table of Contents

Introduction 6

Chapter 1 – The Power Of A Positive Attitude Throughout History 8

Chapter 2 – The Best Ways to Avoid Negative Influences 11

Chapter 3 – Discover How To Easily Change A Negative Attitude Into A Positive Attitude 17

Chapter 4 – Building A Powerful Positive Attitude Foundation 21

Chapter 5 – Morning and Evening Rituals That Will Supercharge Your Life 26

Chapter 6 – Incredible Exercises For A Happy And Positive Attitude 29

Conclusion 33

My Other Books and Audio Books 34

Be sure to check out my website for all my Books and Audio books.

www.AcesEbooks.com

Introduction

I want to thank you and congratulate you for buying the book, "Attitude; Discover the True Power Of A Positive Attitude."

This book contains proven steps and strategies on how to become more positive, likeable and productive using the power of a positive attitude.

It is said that your attitude can make or break you, and this is certainly true. How many people do you know that have a sour attitude? Do you enjoy being around them? Are they successful in life? The answer to these questions is probably a resounding "NO!" People that have a good attitude are happy, live life to its fullest and are most often very successful. They also tend to live longer, be luckier, make more money and have better relationships.

The clinical definition of attitude is: "The learned tendency to evaluate a situation, person, thing, place, issue or event." The way a person perceives these things, creates an attitude. A good example of this is if you were a heavy smoker and were diagnosed with emphysema. Your attitude could be all doom and gloom and you could ask, "Why me?" or just give up and wait to die. If you turn your attitude around, you might say, "Well, now I have no choice but to stop smoking and doing that will make me healthier and my family happy. I will probably get better with time and I will use the money I used to spend on cigarettes on healthy foods instead. This might be an extreme example, but you get the idea.

Attitude is made up of several different components. They are:
1. **Emotion**: how the person, place, thing, etc. makes you feel.
2. **Cognitive**: what you think or believe about the subject.
3. **Behavioral**: how the attitude you have influences your actions and behavior.

Our attitudes start to develop during childhood and they evolve all throughout life. Different experiences or active learning tend to change our attitudes. Attitudes form through our experiences, through observation of situations, through reading, from conversations and seeing the attitudes of others through social interaction and peer pressure.

You might have a teacher you like because you have had good experiences in the classroom with him or her. You've seen this teacher working well with most students in a favorable way, which makes you want to have them as your teacher again. However, one of your friends has had a bad experience with this teacher, which may cloud your attitude and change it a bit so that you avoid the teacher's classes in the future. Who is missing out on some good information and a relationship with a great teacher? You are, because you were influenced by an external source and didn't trust your gut instinct.

The tendency to have a good or bad attitude begins to develop early on, but can change due to a variety of life situations. Having a good attitude does have incredible power. It can give you the will to succeed, the courage to do the right thing and a much friendlier and agreeable person.

A quote from an unknown author with a positive attitude states: "Dear Life: When you give me dilemmas, I make dilemmanade". The more common phrase is: "When life gives you lemons, make lemonade." A situation, thought, place, or thing always has two sides to it and your perspective, or attitude, has much to do with how you handle it.

Good attitudes include:
Happiness
Optimism
Constructive thinking
Creativity
Motivation toward accomplishing goals
Positive thinking

Winston Churchill once said, "Attitude is a little thing that makes a big difference". Positive thinking has the power to change worlds and lives. Let's take a look at how you can nourish a positive attitude in your life so that you can truly be happy and at the top of your game.

Chapter 1 – The Power Of A Positive Attitude Throughout History

"Impossible is a word only to be found in the dictionary of fools." This is a quote from the great leader and warrior Napoleon. Those that have an unstoppable positive attitude can be considered warriors. They don't stop and keep fighting until they succeed or succumb.

Do you think Donald Trump got where he is because he just sat back and took it easy? Mr. Trump had plenty of obstacles to conquer in order to become the mega-businessman he is today. The difference between him and thousands of others in his business, is that he had a never give up attitude and a strong belief in himself.

Many people have become warriors in life in order to become successful. Their attitude played a significant role in their success.

Scott Hamilton, Olympic figure skater, was stricken with cancer, but he did not give in. He said, "The only disability in life is a bad attitude." Scott continues to be a sports commentator for figure skating events. His life may have changed, but he is still a great success story in the world of skating.

Colonel Sanders of Kentucky Fried Chicken fame could have just given up when social security expected him to live on a check for only $105 a month. The man was 65 years old. But instead of whining, he did something about it. He presented his chicken recipe 1009 times and lived in his car traveling all over the USA before someone saw the value and gave him a chance. Anyone else would have quit much sooner and wouldn't have had such a positive attitude.

Albert Einstein, esteemed scientist, never spoke a word until he was 4 years old. Everyone, including his parents, thought he was mentally challenged. He was even expelled from school. He kept rolling along with a positive attitude and eventually won the Nobel Prize and became one of the greatest scientists in all of history.

Walt Disney was a very successful man and creator of Mickey Mouse and the Disney Empire. One of his first positions was as a news editor where he was fired because of lack of creativity. Can you imagine? Walt did not give up. His first business failed in bankruptcy, but his positive attitude carried him through. He pitched his animation idea over 300 times before Mickey Mouse was presented to the world. Now his Disney empire brings untold amounts of joy and happiness to millions of people around the world.

Dr. Suess, one of the most loved children's book authors of all time, was rejected 28 times before he sold his first book. John Grisham, another famous writer, had to make a living as a lawyer for a long time because his first book was rejected 30 times. Stephen King, another famous author, was so disheartened after submitting his first proposal 30 times, he threw the manuscript in the trash. It was his wife who had the positive attitude. She fished it out of the garbage and convinced him to change his attitude. It worked, and since then he has made millions upon millions of dollars. J.K. Rowling, author of the Harry Potter books, was poor, newly divorced and trying to raise a child on her own. She pulled herself out of her depression and published some of the best-loved books on the face of the earth. Her series has made her fabulously wealthy and she is now living the life of her dreams.

Anne Frank once said, "I don't think of all the misery, but of the beauty that still remains." Her Jewish family had to hide from the Germans in attics, basements and behind walls for a long time and this attitude kept them going in the face of insurmountable odds and a grim situation.

Starry, Starry Night is one of the best loved paintings in the world and was created by Vincent Van Gogh. The artist suffered greatly from depression and no wonder. He only sold one painting during his lifetime and that was to a friend. This would have discouraged anyone else, but Van Gogh continued to paint over 800 pieces, which are highly valued to this day.

Ludwig Von Beethoven is a perfect example of a positive attitude warrior. The prolific composer wasn't very good at playing the violin and he hated to practice. His music teachers believed him to be a hopeless case, yet he followed his passion and ended up composing five of the best-loved symphonies the world has ever known and some of them when he was tone deaf.

Winston Churchill never won an election until he was 62 years old and he won a big one; Prime Minister of England. He never stopped trying, even when he failed sixth grade. Abraham Lincoln went to war as a captain and was demoted down to a private before the war was over. He didn't give up and became the President of the United States.

Stephen Spielberg tried very hard to get into the University of Southern California Film School. They would not accept him, much to their chagrin later. He didn't give up. Instead he went to California State University in Long Beach and has gone on to thrill moviegoers across the world with his engaging and top-selling movies.

Thomas Edison, the famous inventor, was not thought to be very intelligent. His teachers told him he was too dumb to learn anything. Once out of school, he was fired twice for being unproductive. Over time his attitude changed and he found that science truly motivated him. He spent all his energy attempting to create a source of light to be used at night besides the traditional candle or fire. He tried 1000 times before he got it right and invented the electric light bulb, one of the greatest inventions of all time. Henry Ford lost everything five times before founding the Ford Corporation. Bill Gates dropped out of college at Harvard and failed in his first business. This positive thinking man is now one of the wealthiest people in the world and has dedicated large amounts of money and resources to eradicating deadly diseases from this planet.

Robert Goddard was a pioneer in liquid-fueled rocket research. At the time, his colleagues and everyone else thought he was nut's trying to explore something that could only happen in a science fiction novel. His attitude gave him the strength to keep going. We wouldn't have the space shuttle today without his initial research. Wernher Von Braun, another space age scientist said, "I have learned to use the word impossible with the greatest caution."

All these positive attitude warriors never quit. They fought until they achieved. That's the true power of a positive attitude! History will be written by those who never gave up, didn't listen to others, believed in themselves and fought with every ounce of their soul and being in order to achieve their goals! Let these famous people inspire and encourage you to do the same.

Chapter 2 – The Best Ways to Avoid Negative Influences

People are influenced everyday by what they experience. People can be influenced by other's comments, things that happen, things they read, things seen on TV, or things picked up on social media. All of these things can have a direct influence on our attitudes, either consciously or subconsciously. It is therefore highly recommended that you avoid negative influences in order to help you keep and maintain a positive attitude.

So, how do we do that when there are negative influences everywhere? It isn't easy, but it is possible.

The person with a positive attitude chooses to be happy, so they have a good attitude and do what it takes to maintain that good attitude. If you do not specifically choose to be a positive person, it is very easy to get sucked into all that negativity that exists out there in the word. It takes work to retain a positive attitude. You may have to eliminate a variety of things or people from your life. Do not think it will be easy. However, if you can maintain a positive attitude, it will bring you rewards without measure.

A wise person once said, "Life is not happening to you. Life is responding to you." - author unknown. This is absolutely true. You dictate what life hands you. If you make up your mind to be successful, odds are, you will be. Maybe not as soon as you would like, but it will happen if you keep pushing forward and never give up.

HANDLING NEGATIVE MEDIA

TV programs, radio, Internet and print news, like newspapers and magazines are all types of media and they are everywhere all day long. It is hard to avoid the media. If you want to know what is going on in the world or community, you have to see some of it. The local and national news are often filled with negativity. I'm not suggesting that you avoid the news and not know what is going on, but you can avoid news programs with an obvious negative or angry perspective. Several political talk show hosts feel as if they need to either whine and complain or blast others right off the face of the earth by persecuting them with angry words. These programs tend to influence their listeners into being discontented, paranoid and just plain mad. Stick to news casts and other programs that are unbiased or ones that report the news without taking sides. These shows just present the facts and you can choose how you feel about what is happening in the world. If you have small children, be careful what is on the TV at news time. The world is already a pretty frightening place and some news stories can frighten young kids. If you are really serious about becoming a positive person, just avoid the news all together. Put your focus onto yourself, your goals and dreams instead of all the crazy stuff happening around the globe. Put on some relaxing music, meditate, exercise, read some positive affirmations, review your goals, play with your pets or kids, read some uplifting books, chances are you really won't be missing much by skipping the news.

NEGATIVE PEOPLE AND RELATIONSHIPS

Good reasons to stay away from negative people and relationships include:

1. Your attitude is influenced by the people you interact with every day. Negative people bring you down with them. It is important to get out in the world and see new things and meet new people. If your friends do not want to do that, you might want to think about keeping those friends. You would be surprised at all the positivity in the world when you go looking for it. There is a reason that people from big name schools tend to be much more successful. Steel sharpens steel. If you are surrounded by whiners, complainers, liars, excuse makers, or a whole variety of other people who try to slide by instead of doing what is necessary to succeed, you will find yourself in a much more difficult position to succeed in. If you can't find positive people in real life, there are plenty of people on the internet. There are plenty of great groups out there that focus on the positive. Search for those groups.

    Go ahead and search for new friends and weed out those who hold you back or drain your energy and try to find the positive and uplifting souls on this planet. It only takes a few great people that you can connect with on a regular basis to make a huge difference in your life. Another word for good friends like this are accountability partners. These are people who are positive and try and hold you to a higher standard to accomplish your goals and dreams. Keep on searching until you a have some good people to work with and you may be shocked at just how much more motivated and productive you are! You can also be proactive and get a larger group of people like this together, called a mastermind group, where you all work together to succeed. Facebook is great for creating groups like this.

2. Negative people and attitudes lead you away from successful goals. Have you ever told someone what your dreams were and they just shrugged and said something like, "Good luck with that." A good friend with a positive attitude would listen, comment and give you some good feedback, while a negative friend would either ignore your dream or knock it down. A good friend will help you obtain your goals and encourage you. A negative friend can do a variety of damaging things that could help discourage you from achieving your dreams and goals.

3. A toxic relationship is not only toxic to your attitude, but it is toxic to your health and can make you sick. It is not easy to do sometimes, but this is

where you need to be a hero and heroine and write your own destiny and control who or what has influence in your life.

4. Positive people tend to exercise, eat right and are generally healthier than their negative counterparts. If something is wrong with them, they immediately know and seek help. Negative people tend to feel bad all the time and don't know when to get help. They might become a couch potato and rarely exercise. They may consume processed foods and junk food instead of creating healthy meals. If you spend a great deal of time around someone like this, it is likely you will eat the same food and do the same things.

HOW TO HANDLE NEGATIVITY AT WORK

The workplace is a petri dish of negativity. In some companies it runs rampant and you may have to leave your job and find another one in order to maintain your positive attitude. There are plenty of workplaces out there that strive to create a positive attitude for their employees and those are the ones that are super successful. There are plenty of jobs that can survive with a terrible boss who rules by threatening to fire rather than trying to build a team of superstars. Years ago finding a job was somewhat easy to do, but today jobs are few and far between in many areas of the work force, allowing for negative businesses to get by. Although finding your dream job can be difficult to do, it is crucial for your overall happiness. For more help on finding what truly makes you happy in this life, be sure to check out my book on: Personal Growth.

Here are some ways to try and keep a positive attitude at work:

1. Pay attention to the atmosphere the minute you walk into the building. Did the receptionist say good morning to you or did she grunt at you and continue complaining to another coworker? If you see it isn't a good day, lock yourself in your office, take a deep breath, get grounded and start thinking positive thoughts. As you focus on your goals for the day, unlock the door. You are now prepared. You can even make it a goal to be able to work from home. This is what I was able to do, which allowed me to control my environment, which allowed me to design my day according to what works best for me, not what works best for some giant corporation. It also allowed me to control a huge amount of other aspects in my life, which can really give you the edge if you are serious about trying hard and living a productive and healthy life. Just being able to wake up when I want, not have to drive to work, exercise when I want, super hydrate myself when I want, work when I want, stretch when I want, eat when I want, socialize when I want and all according to a strategy of goals that I am working on that have been put in order of importance really is a tremendous advantage! If working for someone else just isn't your thing, make it a goal to find out what will truly make you happy and successful!

2. Let any negative words bounce off you as if you were wearing a golden suit of magical armor that deflects all negativity.

3. If a coworker comes to you with a bad attitude, listen, be kind and suggest things they can do to make it better. Don't dwell on it or let it drag you down. If they keep doing it, let them know that although you love/like them, they really need to tone it down a bit so that you can continue to move forward. Life can be hard. Try not to let it be harder than it has to be by dragging around the weight of other people's problems in your head. Another good reason to avoid the daily news!

4. If you start having negative thoughts, keep them to yourself. Don't spread the bad vibes all over the office. If it gets to be overwhelming, take to a good friend or mentor and get some good advice as to how to proceed.

5. Stay neutral in group situations and avoid engaging in the gossip. You might want to rescue someone who has a severe negative attitude, but think about it first. Are you going to be able to change their perspective or will they think you are butting in where you don't belong? Sometimes it is just better to combat negativity slowly, so don't stop saying good morning to the receptionist in the morning. Eventually she might smile and say good morning back to you because of your good influence. It can take a tremendous amount of time and effort to get someone to finally come around. Give it your best, but don't waste too much time and energy on people like this. Focus on what you need to do! It's easy to be negative... it's hard to be positive, a champion, someone who will do what the other people won't do in order to succeed!

Be sure to check out this great YouTube video by Barbara Glanz on how handle coworkers in the workplace, Keeping a positive attitude in a negative workplace.

HOW TO HANDLE NEGATIVE INDIVIDUALS

If you can eliminate negative people from your life, go for it. Sometimes your negative friends aren't worth keeping. However, if you can't bring yourself to end a relationship or if the negative person is a family member, getting rid of them is easier said than done.

Close Friends and Family
Feel free to ask close friends and family members why they are so negative. You owe it to them to find out the reason. There may be a very good reason for their negative attitude and you might be able to help. You can butt in to the lives of close friends and family without having to worry because you are closer to these people than anyone else. Just remember that this is your life! Not theirs. If they don't believe in you, support you, give you good advice or are just not on the same wavelength as you, then you need to do what you need to do in order to accomplish your dream life! Close friends and family can be your greatest asset

or biggest of nightmares. At some point, you need to decide what you stand for, what you are going to tolerate and what amount of loyalty and respect you are going to demand from your relationships so that you can fulfill you life's purpose. Of course, to be able to get this type of loyalty and respect, you need to be the type of person who deserves it through working hard. This is summed up nicely by the one and only Arnold Schwarzenegger in the YouTube video, Six Secrets to Success (New), posted by Travis Fisher.

Acquaintances
A relationship break with an acquaintance would be difficult, but not earth shattering. You need to decide if a relationship with the negative person is worth the trouble. Try maintaining your positive attitude and it may rub off on them. If it doesn't, rethink the relationship and break it off if you have to. To be best in the world, it isn't easy. All the great sports teams have to cut people until they are left with the best they can possibly get. You need to do the same in your life.

Coworkers
Focus on the good qualities of coworkers and try to ignore the bad. You have to relate to these people or find another job where there could be a whole new batch of "negative Nancy's." Stay away from office politics, wear you headphones and play music or paste positive quotes around the office. They will get the idea eventually and leave you alone. If you are looking for a Leadership position, then take charge, let them know they are acting like losers and that if you want to win, they need to get their act together!

TRY A LITTLE MEDITATION

Some people find it easier to deal with all those negative influences when they engage in a little meditation. You can do a meditation session in the morning, so you are ready for whatever comes, or you can take a moment mid-day to recharge positive feelings, or you can wait until after work and around bedtime so that you have sweet dreams. You can meditate once a day or several times per day. It just depends on what you need to keep that positive attitude. Your session doesn't have to take a long time. It can be as short as 5 to 10 minutes to help infuse yourself with positive energy.

Some things you can mediate on are quotes and sayings that exude positivity. You can find a picture of a person you admire for their positive attitude. It can be the Dalai Lama all the way to your Uncle Joe. Pull out that photo and look into the person's eyes. Thank them for their example and try to see the troubles of the day through their eyes. What would they think and what would they do? Maybe you had a disagreement with a coworker about overstepping boundaries. The Dalai Lama may say, "In the big scheme of things, does this really matter?" Meditate on what they would tell you to do to prevent the situation from occurring again.

If nothing has happened truly negative throughout the day, you are very lucky. Thank the universe or your higher power for a great day. If some negativity did creep into your day, but there was nothing you could have done about it, resolve to move on. Here is a great YouTube video on meditation by meditationrelaxclub, Healing Spirit: Guided Meditation for Relaxation, Anxiety, Depression and Self Acceptance.

Please see Chapter 5 of this book for more information on morning and evening rituals that keep you positive throughout the day.

MOVING AWAY FROM NEGATIVITY

When people around you start complaining, show them kindness. It is hard to keep whining when you are in the presence of a kind and gracious person. If you keep up that attitude, you will find that people will stop complaining when they are around you.

Avoid joining in on the negativity. If a coworker starts bashing the boss about a decision he or she made, regale that person with all the good things the boss has done.

Be constructive and suggest to the negative person things that will make the situation better. If Aunt Mary is being negative about Uncle Bob because he never does anything around the house, talk to Uncle Bob. He may not know Aunt Mary is dissatisfied. He might need a little push in the right directions.

If you find yourself in a negative mood, be sure to check out this YouTube video by Nick Vujicic, The Motivational Speaker with No Arms and No Legs – Nick Vujicic, to put your reality on this planet in perspective.

CLEAN UP YOUR ENVIRONMENT

A clean, neat environment invites positivity. Get rid of junk and purge your surroundings of all unnecessary things. Organize your life and you will be much more effective. Take a good look at what you watch on TV or movies, what video games you play, the friends you keep and so on. Sometimes it is better purge all of these negative sources from your life.

Bill Meyer said, "Every thought is like a seed. If you plant crab apples, don't count on harvesting Golden Delicious."

See what kind of attitudes you can cultivate in your community, family or workplace just by planting the right seed and pulling out those weeds. Encourage others to accomplish their goals and dreams, and if they are a true friend, they will return the favor.

Chapter 3 – Discover How To Easily Change A Negative Attitude Into A Positive Attitude

An unknown author once said, "If we try to see something positive in everything we do, life won't necessarily become easier, but it will become more valuable."

There are two sides to every situation. You can either look at a glass half empty or a glass half full. If you think of it as a glass half full then you have a more positive outlook. Most people and things can be classified as being good or bad and most times you can come up with a good slant if you look hard enough. Thinking in a positive manner (the glass is half full) helps us to take on the world and prevents us from giving up. It is all in the perspective.

CHANGE THEORIES

Several theories exist that can help change a negative attitude into a positive one. In the learning theory, the subject has a positive emotional response to certain things because good things happen when the situation or thing is in action. An example of this is the baseball player who has to wear the beaten up, smelly and overused baseball hat to all the big games because he has had good luck with it and he associates it with victory. The team doesn't win because of the hat, but it may win because of the increased productivity of the player who believes in and wears the hat. The positive attitude is learned from an emotional response. Learning theory is directed by personal experience or by observing others.

When someone persuades you to think differently or change your attitude, the elaboration theory is at work. In this theory, change occurs because you are motivated to listen and think about the situation. This is similar to choosing a political candidate. You may start out supporting one candidate, but after a debate or TV commercial, you might change your mind to support the other one.

Dissonance theory is a difficult one. A person might have some very strong beliefs in something and in order to change their mind or attitude, they must set aside these beliefs. Someone with a Christian background may have a difficult time if their son tells them he is gay. They may struggle for a while with the belief that homosexuality is thought of as a sin according to their religion, but they might side-line that belief because they love their son and they may believe that God may have a greater plan.

These theories all work to change an attitude.

MENTAL CHANGES

Mental change can help to change a negative attitude to a positive one. The following are some of those mental changes:

1. Literally, take control of your brain and force yourself to find something positive about a person or situation. A person I know has been going to college on and off for six years in order to get a library science degree. During her last year of school she developed a problem with her eyes and became partially blind. Her vision was limited so much that she could not read. Most people would have given up and quit school, but she went on to learn braille and is pursuing a career as a teacher and librarian for the blind. She didn't quit. She took control and did something about the situation.

2. Stop living in the past or dwelling on the future. The present is here and now, so don't miss a minute of it. The past cannot change, but you control the present and that affects the future. Make the best of it. Although this may seem like a simple paragraph in an eBook, it is one of the most important things that you can ever master for happiness and a great attitude through life. Learn how to live in the "Now" for increased happiness and positive attitude. Check out this YouTube video by Eric Tran of Oprah Winfrey interviewing Eckhart Tolle about the Power of Now, [Eckhart Tolle Interview With Oprah The Power of Now YouTube](), to truly realize the power of living in the moment!

3. Avoid negative words like "can't" or "won't". Using the words "can" and "will" gives your brain a shift and you will actually start to think in a positive manner. There is something to that children's story, "The Little Train that Could". In the story the little train experienced a big hill and he made it up that hill just by saying the iconic words, "I think I can," over and over again and never giving up! I can't tell you how many successful people have been superstars just because they just never gave up. They never gave up on a play, they never gave up on a day, they never gave up on their beliefs, they never gave up on themselves and they just kept on pushing forward. Some people call it heart, others will, and other tenacity, but what it all boils down to is developing an unwavering belief in yourself and your goals and then just moving towards them every day while never giving in. Some days will be better than others, but that desire to keep moving forward is something all the great ones throughout history have had.

4. Many people have a hard time accepting change, but without change life would be very boring. Accept change and make a new strategy. Remember when things change, there is always an opportunity for great success for those who look for it.

5. The power of attitude is not always understood. Negative attitudes foster anxiety, anger, bitterness and envy. When those emotions take hold, you might make some negative decisions that can affect your life adversely. If you choose to remain positive, the likelihood of making a decision that can enhance your life is very good. When you have a positive attitude, your

reactions tend to be positive. If your child is misbehaving, you will tend to handle the situation with more compassion and with more kindness if you have a positive attitude. The same holds true for a variety of other situations that may come up in your life.

WATCH OUT FOR NEGATIVITY

The following items are things you need to watch out for in order to keep positive and to not slip into a negative thought or action:

1. The brain has a habit of slipping negative thoughts into your head. Ignore them. It is natural to have worries, but you do not have to dwell on them. If you do, they tend to look more serious than they really are.

2. Find the silver lining. Always try to find something good. Maybe Uncle Pete has a problem with alcohol, but maybe he is also a kind hearted soul who just needs a little help.

3. Remember that sometimes an event that turns out less than what was expected, can still lead to something good. Do the best you can with the situation. I was at a wedding reception held in a park. Part of the reception was held under tents while the other was in an enclosed and very small pavilion. The wind blew up and rain fell in sheets causing all the guests to pile in the crowded pavilion. Then the electricity went out. The bride and groom took it in stride. Candles were lit and some other friends lit the area with their cell phones. The food was served and was mostly hot and the guitarist from the band pulled out his acoustic guitar and we still could dance. It was all very romantic and quite beautiful.

4. Lighten up! Avoid taking yourself so seriously. If you lessen your ego, you become less paranoid and enjoy life more. Be sure to check out a fan favorite book of mine for more details on this: Laughter and Humor Therapy.

5. Accept trials and tribulations; they make us what we are. Do you think you would learn without having difficulties? Anything worth having has to be worked for or fought for. Learning to deal with a difficult boss gives you the ability to become a great leader if only to learn what not to do.

A study conducted at Stanford Research Institute showed 87.5 percent of success comes from **attitude** and a mere 12.5 percent from knowledge and abilities. Attitude has great power and changing from a negative attitude to a positive one will have more influence than is comprehensible. The famous saying is more true than you can imagine "It only takes one bad apple to spoil the bunch."

To be more positive, check out this very old Italian proverb which states, "Since the house is on fire, let us warm ourselves." Sure, the house is burning down, but at least we are warm.

If you have problems changing your attitude, you might want to read several of my other e-books. I have written books on Happiness, Inspiration, Motivation, Ultimate Health and Personal Growth that will give you some great suggestions to help you become a mighty hero/heroine in this life. Another one of my bestselling books on Habit can help you to easily make good positive habits and explain in great detail how to eliminate bad habits.

Chapter 4 – Building A Powerful Positive Attitude Foundation

It is one thing to change perspective and attitude and another to build it up so that you do not revert back to a negative perspective.

Will Foley was a major league baseball player that was active in the late 1800's and he played for several teams including the Cincinnati Reds and the Milwaukee Grays. He said, "The world is full of cactus, but we don't have to sit on it." This gives you a humorous insight into how he felt about a positive attitude and he was spot on. The negativity is always out there, but we do not have to participate in it. By building a positive attitude, you will be able to succeed at what you do and have a better life.

POSITIVE AFFIRMATIONS
Chapter 5 of this book has many suggestions for positive affirmations and how to use them in a morning or evening ritual. Affirmations are words and sentences that you say to yourself in order to convince your mind to think or do something. Some examples of positive affirmations are:
- I deserve to be happy.
- I am smart enough and organized enough to be able to get a good paying job.
- I am worthy of love.
- I see the good in all people and situations.
- I love my life.
- I am generous, giving and caring every day of my life.
- I act quickly and decisively.
- I am going to be a winner today.
- I will improve myself every day by following good habits, eating healthy and promoting good relationships in my life.
- I am super strong, healthy, wealthy and wise.
- I am super creative and perform flawlessly.
- The list goes on and on! Be sure to make your own personalized affirmations that pertain to you and the goals that you have in your life.

Affirmations build confidence within your positive attitude. If you tell yourself you can do it, you are more likely to be able to complete the task. I knew a teacher that worked at an inner city high school where the kids were very unruly and were unlikely to succeed. Teachers dropped like flies at the school because they just couldn't handle the discipline problems. My friend was a tiny woman, someone very unlikely to succeed at this school. She walked in everyday with her head held high and each morning would start the day with a set of positive affirmations done with the kids in her homeroom. She would start every class with these affirmations by saying them and having the students repeat them back to her. Some of the affirmations she used were:

- I will be kind to my fellow students and my teachers
- I will learn something new today
- I deserve a good education
- I can succeed if I try

The kids thought it was pretty stupid at first and many mocked her and her affirmations, but she kept it up and did not waiver. Pretty soon the kids were repeating her affirmations and calling out their own for the class to repeat. She rarely had trouble with the students and if anyone wanted to do any harm to her, they didn't stand a chance. She was at that school 25 years before she retired and changed the lives of many inner city students.

FORGIVE

Forgiveness releases hard feelings and bitterness that might be held in the heart and that is a main source of a negative attitude. Asking for forgiveness is a great relief, even if the person you wronged is apprehensive. Forgiving others is difficult to do, but not as hard as forgiving yourself. Find out how to expertly forgive with my book devoted totally to the subject: Forgiveness. The nice thing is, you don't even have to tell the person or circumstance that you forgive them; you can just do it and move on. This is another subject that is easily said and not so easily done. I would also recommend checking out the variety of free "Tapping" videos on YouTube as they can be quite helpful. I am also going to highly recommend HypnosisDownloads and the downloads of: Forgive and Move On as well as the download Let It Go. Then, if you really want to try even harder, you can use the forgiveness subliminal on: Subliminal Power2 on your choice electronic device.

Confucius said, "To be wronged is nothing unless you continue to remember it." This tells us it is an old practice to forgive and forget in order to live on. This is something I have struggled with myself, that's why I was able to find the best resources for you to utilize in order to be happy, get a good attitude and move on.

INVENTORY OF YOUR LIFE

Keeping a running inventory on certain aspects of your life can help to build positive attitude. Purchase a plastic recipe box and put in recipe cards that fit inside. Create three different life inventory boxes to give you inspiration and help you stay positive. If you don't want to use a physical box, then substitute the box for a nice digital program like OneNote or Evernote. I personally use OneNote and love it, although I hear Evernote is great as well. Or, another of my favorite techniques, is to use a digital video recorder to record all my thoughts, then organize them on the computer according to category.

1. **MEMORY INVENTORY** – Fill this box with good memories by writing them down on index cards. Use memories that give you peace and are just

plain happy. You can even file them under a subject like kids, mom, pets, vacations, etc. Perhaps you had a dog when you were growing up. He was your constant companion and made you happy. Make a card and include a picture if you have one. Write down memories of this pet and file them away.

2. **GRATITUDE INVENTORY** – Write a card for each thing that inspires gratitude in your life. Is it your job, your children, your spouse, a hobby, friends or something else? You will be amazed at how many good things you have in your life once you sit down and think about it and you will be more amazed at how thinking about them improves your attitude.

3. **INSPIRATION INVENTORY** – For your personal inventory, keep cards with inspirational thoughts, phrases or quotes on them. Also detail those people, both ones you know and ones you don't, that inspire you and why they do.

These inventories come in handy when you feel down and not so positive. Just pull one out and start looking through it to get a boost of positivity. This may not seem so important now, but you will regret it if you don't do it. This is one thing that I have done throughout my life and I really enjoy going back and viewing all my great victories and accomplishments. I have a huge music, video, audio, and journalistic diary of all the great events in my life as well as a whole library of uplifting books, pictures, computer programs, etc. from the greatest authors and people in history. When things seem down, I can always retreat to my base foundation and just read back all the great accomplishments in my life. I don't want to brag, but I have the heart of a lion, great genetics and the will and determination to win no matter what the sacrifice and I have been fortunate enough to have great mentors like Arnold Schwarzenegger and Tony Robbins... so I have had a lot of glorious victories in my life! It's not all been a cake walk though... let me be clear. Winners will do what others will not, and the majority of that time it just boils down to the fact that smart choice and hard work pays off. But, however many victories you have had in your life, be sure to record it! Record the things that make you the happiest and in the future you will have it at your fingertips to review whenever you need that extra boost!

VISION BOARDS

A vision board is a visual depiction of all your dreams and goals in life. You can use poster board, magazine pictures, drawings, quotes, photos and words to make the vision board. If you have aspirations of becoming a millionaire, you could put it on your vision board. You could put in a picture of your beautiful mansion or of a huge pile of cash that you have at your disposal. Those that desire to travel can paste pictures of sights they want to see on their vision board. If you dream of having your own restaurant, put the floor plan on the board along with photos of other restaurants you would like emulate and some of the equipment you would need to start your restaurant. Also include a copy of your menu. Those that want to have a family complete with a house with a white picket fence can put pictures of that on their vision board. Put whatever you want on the vision board. Remember, you can make a digital vision board as well, simply by pasting your favorite pictures into a document.

Vision boards can consist of a single goal or many. You can also have more than one vision board at a time. **The key to your visualizations is to use high emotion while visualizing!**

Place the completed vision board on a wall where you can see it every day and take the time to look at it and visualize what your life would be like if the dreams on the board came true. A friend of mine made his vision board on a trifold science fair board that was rigid and stood up by itself. He wanted to start his own business that would be very successful. He placed a floor plan of his store on the board, samples of what he would sell, pictures of equipment he would need and a list of personnel needs his store would have to have. He placed it on a table next to his bed and would turn on his side so he could see the board every night before he turned off the light. He visualized a day of running his business for about a half hour before sleep overtook him. Five years later he owns a popular computer repair and sales store and is very successful. His vision board fostered a positive attitude that made his dreams come to fruition. Cesar L. Rodriguez has a great YouTube video on vision boards called How to make a Vision Board. Visit that video and get very good ideas on making your own.

TALK TO YOURSELF

Your biggest critic is yourself, but on the other hand, your best supporter is also yourself. Everyone has that subtle inner voice that calls out to us and gives us advice. It is very wise to listen to that voice and to talk to it out loud. People may wonder if you've gone off the deep end when you talk to yourself, but some of the most positive people in the world seek advice, listen to and talk to themselves. The only one you can really depend on to keep your positive attitude is yourself. This activity is most commonly called "Self-Talk." Here is a YouTube video of Dr. Ivan Joseph delivering a fascinating lecture about Self-Talk called The skill of self confidence at the TEDx conference at Ryerson University in 2012.

VOLUNTEER

If you have a bad attitude about your life, change it by volunteering at the local food bank, animal shelter, homeless shelter, home for battered women or a soup kitchen. Helping others that are down on their luck improves your attitude and shows you there are others worse off than you are. Merely giving a helping hand in times of trouble will help your attitude build up to a big positive one. Most communities have many different volunteer situations. They are usually advertised in the local newspaper but you can also contact your local chamber of commerce for other volunteer ideas.

STOP LOOKING FOR FLAWS

Some people just can't help themselves. Even in a positive situation they are hell bent on finding flaws in everything. Humanity is flawed. People are going to make mistakes. Some people are going to take it too far. They may use humor to belittle others in order to increase their standing in the group. Don't be that person. Be the hero/heroine, the person that people can rely on, the person that people know can get the job done. Instead of playing into other peoples petty games, look for people's strengths, look for allies that you can go to battle with. My advice... look for loyalty. Mighty kingdoms have been won based on loyalty and trust.

SWITCH FRIENDS

In order to build up a positive attitude it may be necessary to end friendships and begin others. Make a list of your friends and the benefits of each of them. If there are little to no benefits, you may need a change. Make new friends with positive attitudes. Meet them in positive places like community events, church, support groups, the internet, or places where people of like minds get together. If you have a dog, visit the dog park to find friends that also have dogs. If you like to sing, join a choir and get to know the people there. If you like to read, join a book club and participate. If you enjoy self-improvement, research a good Facebook group for that. Avoid negative places like night clubs and bars.

Building up a positive attitude takes some work with some people. Maintaining it also takes work, but the benefits are great.

Chapter 5 – Morning and Evening Rituals That Will Supercharge Your Life

Many people find their lives enhanced by performing a morning and/or evening ritual. A ritual is a certain succession of actions that help reinforce beliefs and attitudes.

What kind of attitude would you foster if every morning you wok up, turned off the alarm and grumbled when you had to get up? Surprisingly, or maybe not so surprisingly, this is what most people do. They would rather dream the day away in bed than meet it head long in order to reach and touch their dreams. How much better would their day go if they woke up with a smile ready to take on whatever came?

Rituals do not have to take much time. Waking up 15 to 20 minutes early is all you really need unless you want to incorporate physical exercise, a shower and getting ready.

I personally started doing my new morning routine several months ago and I have noticed a huge difference in not only my productivity, but my overall energy levels and happiness as well! To go along with that, my attitude has been great!

Check out the following suggestions on how to foster a positive attitude with a morning ritual:

1. As soon as consciousness seeps in; smile. Stretch those lips in an upward position to start your day off right.

2. Breathe deep. This will get your blood circulating and start pumping blood through those muscles that have been relaxed and dormant all night long. Lie on your back and place your hands on your stomach under you ribs. Breathe in slowly and deliberately, preferably through your nose. As you breathe in, your stomach should puff out a bit. Your shoulders should not rise. Hold the breathe and breath out through your lips like you are blowing out a candle. Do this as slow as you can. While you breathe out, your stomach near your ribs should suck in again. Take about 5 good breaths thinking only about breathing in and out.

3. Once breathing is achieved, think of three or four things you are most grateful for. It can be your family, your job, your pet or anything else. This should only take a few moments.

4. Breathe in and out quickly about 10 times. This should clear your head and get you ready to start moving.

5. Stretch your muscles starting at your neck and move down to your shoulders, your arms, your hands, your back and chest, your hips, your stomach, your thighs, your legs and your feet. If you need to sit up to do this, do so. Once you get good at doing this you will want to think of a single goal or several that you wish to achieve while you stretch. Don't dwell on them though, but get out of bed and take care of your needs.

6. Go to the kitchen and drink a full glass of water. You can then exercise if you wish or start the shower. The water will get your digestive system ready to meet the day.

7. While in the shower start your litany of positive affirmations. These are phrases that accomplish a goal or just make you feel good. Repeating positive affirmations is a method of self-hypnosis. If you keep saying it, you are affirming it and you will believe it. The following are some good general positive affirmations to start your day:

    - I will have a great day today
    - I will learn something new today
    - I will help someone in need
    - I will be strong in the face of adversity
    - I will be kind to others
    - I deserve to be happy
    - I will do all in my power to stay healthy
    - I will do my work to the best of my abilities
    - I will do something to improve my life today
    - I will make progress toward my goals and dreams
    - I will take what comes today and deal with it the best that I can
    - I will make good decisions today
    - I will eat healthy today and not be tempted
    - I will be successful today
    - I will be confident

You can also affirm your goals during the affirmation stage of the morning ritual. I would affirm being a successful writer that could live off the money I make from writing. A business person might affirm becoming president of their company in five years. A teacher may affirm that he or she would reach the students in class so that they learn and are successful.

Take a few more breathes and go out there to meet the day with a smile on your face and bounce in your step.

Bonus Ideas For Morning Ritual

1. Don't check your email within 30 minutes of waking up in the morning! If you ignore your email and do your morning ritual first,

statistics show that you are over 30% more likely to be more productive during that day.
2. Read for fifteen minutes from a self-development or similarly uplifting source of information.
3. Listen to favorite music while stretching or doing yoga for 20 minutes or so.
4. Review all of your goals and then visualize yourself doing and accomplishing them with emotion!
5. Making a strategic plan that has you doing the most important things first in the day and then finishing everything else after that.
6. Having a nutritious meal early in the day. One of my favorites is organic baby spinach and a banana mixed in my Nutribullet blender to make a delicious and energizing smoothie.

Your evening ritual, should you choose to do it, should focus on calming the body and mind in order to ready it for sleep while still fostering a positive attitude.

Here are a few steps you can follow to perform an evening ritual:

1. Do some deep breathing. Deep breathing does waken the body, but it also induces relaxation. Lie in the bed and slowly breathe in and out, as you did in the morning. Do this five to six times concentrating only on the breaths you are taking. Quiet the mind of everything else.

2. Set your alarm and think about your day. Evaluate progress toward goals and think of three things you did during that day that fulfilled your morning affirmations.

3. If you pray, say your evening prayers. If you do not pray, reinforce some of your favorite affirmations.

4. Have a good night's sleep.

If you have problems thinking up your own affirmations, view this YouTube video by Jason Stephenson, Law of Attraction Positive Affirmations for Success and Abundance, Live a Prosperous Life. Also check out the next chapter for some links to some excellent videos on Positive Affirmation Meditations.

Chapter 6 – Incredible Exercises For A Happy And Positive Attitude

This book has been filled with activities and exercises that you can do to enhance a positive attitude, but in this chapter we will expound on some of the things you have already done and learn some new things to do. I have also included video links that you can watch in order to enhance your attitude and I have also included my web site for my other books that will also help you to keep a great attitude and become successful in life.

VISION BOARD EXERCISES

We've already learned how to make a vision board and some suggestions were given on how to use it. If your vision board does not exemplify where you want to be in five to ten years, then change it. Prioritize steps that are needed to reach that dream. Write them down and then memorize them. That way it will etch into your brain. Memorize your steps at least three times a week and the steps will come naturally to you even when you are out in the community and one of the steps crops up. Pretty soon you will realize you have been taking your steps all along without even thinking about it. If you achieve your vision on your board, make a new one with a new goal. In order to stay positive you should always have a goal to achieve and challenge you. Don't be afraid to strike when the opportunity arises. You deserve success... strive for it and take it whenever the opportunity presents itself.

STRIVE TO BE NICE EXERCISE

It is much easier to have a good attitude if you are a nice person. Those with sour dispositions rarely have anything but a bad attitude. Choose to do something nice for someone every day. Maybe the person in front of you at Starbucks doesn't have enough cash in their pockets for their coffee. Pull out a buck and give it to them. Maybe the kids down the road lost their ball in the high grass at the end of the street. Go find it for them or get them a new one. Your wife or husband may be having a rough morning and just can't get things together. Offer to help them out. The smallest thing you do that makes someone else smile will improve your attitude and theirs as well.

AFFIRMATION EXERCISES AND ACTIVITY

Get a book of quotes from the library and find ones from famous people that support a good attitude. Write them down in a notebook, computer, scrapbook or on note cards. Here are a few to start you out.

"Those who wish to sing, always find a song" - Swedish Proverb

"If we shall take the good we find, asking no questions, we shall have heaping measures." - Ralph Waldo Emerson

"If you don't get everything you want, think of the things you don't get that you don't want." - Oscar Wilde

"Oh my friend, it's not what they take away from you that counts. It's what you do with what you have left." - Hubert Humphrey

"In the depth of winter I finally learned that there was in me an invincible summer" - Albert Camus

I know a man who founded a very successful drug and alcohol rehabilitation facility. He has, in his top drawer, a quote written on an index card. Every morning, when he comes to work, he opens that drawer to retrieve his pen. The quote is right there to remind him to be compassionate and kind and to do the best he can every day. He has been doing this for about 45 years.

ATTITUDE CHECK EXERCISE

You can do this exercise alone, but it is much better to ask a trusted confidant to help you. If you have the aid of someone else, who will be blatantly honest, pick a word or words you both will recognize as a signal word. Choose a word that would not normally pop up in general conversation. It might be the word "dragon" or "red zone". When you start complaining and fretting with a negative attitude, your friend should say the signal word. This should immediately signal you to stop, take a look at what you are saying and it also signals you to change your thoughts to something more positive.

If you are doing this on your own, it is a bit more difficult. You will have to recognize that you have slipped into negativity and sometimes we just don't see that in ourselves.

Keep track of how many times you slip up and strive to do better the next week.

JOURNALING

One of the best ways to be able to look back on your progress to becoming a more positive person is to start a journal. You don't have to take the time to write every night. Once every few days can do the trick. Actually, once most people start to journal, they enjoy it so much they want to write something in it almost every day. There is something strangely cathartic about writing down your feelings, strategies, goals and experiences. In your journal you may want to write what you did to stay positive. You may want to keep a record of goals and achievements or explain a situation when you slip up. You might want to record happy times during the week. You can look back on your journal to see your progress or refer to it when a similar situation comes up where you either handled it positively, or didn't. You can track your diet, so that you know what the best foods and supplements are for your optimum performance. A physical journal is great for this, or your can use a digital program like OneNote or Evernote.

PHYSICAL EXERCISE AND ATTITUDE

Endorphins are those things that release in your body during exercise that make you feel good. They are supreme mood enhancers and they help you to stay positive. We usually think of endorphins being released after very high energy physical exercise, but some studies indicate that enough endorphins are released during low intensity exercise. If you can engage in high energy exercise, go for it and release those mood enhancing endorphins. If you can't, engage in yoga, light running or walking or swim. Just 10 minutes of exercise that you enjoy doing will release enough to give you a more positive attitude. But ideally you should strive for at least 20 minutes on a daily basis.

POSITIVE ATTITUDE BOOKS

Many of my self-development books coincide with having a positive attitude. Go to my website by clicking here and see if you are interested in the following e-books. Some of my fan favorites are:

- Forgiveness
- Confidence
- Motivation
- Habit
- Inspirational
- Productivity
- Self-Discipline
- Personal Growth
- Overcome Fear
- Goals and Dreams
- Subliminal Power

HELPFUL VIDEOS

The Internet has a plethora of helpful YouTube videos that explain and enhance a positive attitude. Here are some very good ones that are very informative and enjoyable:

- Positive Mindset Tips 5 – How to Develop a Positive Mindset by Work Life Balance by Work Life Balance.
- Life Coaching Skills – A Positive Attitude – Career and Life Coach by Dieter Pauwels.

- Positive Affirmations – Meditation Part 1: by thereachapproach. This explains how affirmations work and Positive Affirmations – Meditation Part 2 is the actual meditation.
- 3 Words that can Change Your Life Forever by Brian Tracy – shows that using three neutral words work wonders rather than using negative words.
- Change Your Attitude – Walter Bond by Primeau TV
- Attitude Slideshow by boytown999's channel
- Positive Thinking Meditation: Endorphin Meditation with Positive Affirmations by Linda Hall

Enjoy these videos, books, advice, insights, strategies and all the exercises included that will help you become a positive and successful person! Remember it's your life! You design the course and you control your own destiny! Don't forget the past, but don't let it control you either. Forgive and move on. Fortune favors the brave. Focus on the positive, live in the now, and move forward with will and conviction. Get some loyal and trustworthy friends, believe in yourself, strive to do what is right and move forward with purpose and conviction. I believe in you always.

Conclusion

I hope this book was able to help you to gain a positive attitude and use its power to become successful in your life.

The next step is to try to become a more positive person on a daily basis by utilizing your favorite strategies from this book. Everything you do that creates a more positive atmosphere, makes you a better and more successful person able to reach goals and be a respected person in the community. Wouldn't you love to be the person that everyone looks up to? Wouldn't you love to be happy almost every day of your life? Wouldn't you like to wake up every morning and know there is something good in store for you? That's the true power of a positive attitude!

The benefits of having a positive attitude include:

- It helps you achieve your goals and attain success.
- You will tend to have more happiness in your life.
- You tend to have more energy to deal with what the day brings.
- It can increase your faith in all your skills and abilities.
- You will tend to have more hope for the future.
- You are much more likely to inspire and motivate others.
- Obstacles may still come, but you will tend to be better equipped to deal with them.
- You will tend to get more respect from those you know and those who follow you.
- You will tend to give more smiles and get more smiles in return.

The choice of what type of attitude you want to have for your life is yours. It's never easy. The winner's in life tend to be made up of the people who are willing to make the hard choices and do the hard work. But in the end, when they are sitting in victory lane, it is all worth it. How bad do you want to have a happy and productive life? You now know exactly some things that you can easily incorporate into your life to increase your success potential. Be sure to utilize them with an iron will and a conviction that you will succeed, that you will be positive and that nothing is going to stop your greatness from blessing this world!

Finally, if you discovered at least one thing that has helped you or that you think would be beneficial to someone else, be sure to take a few seconds to easily post a quick positive review. As an author, your positive feedback is desperately needed. Your highly valuable five star reviews are like a river of golden joy flowing through a sunny forest of mighty trees and beautiful flowers! *To do your good deed in making the world a better place by helping others with your valuable insight, just leave a nice review.*

My Other Books and Audio Books
www.AcesEbooks.com

Peak Performance Books

Health Books

Be sure to check out my audio books as well!

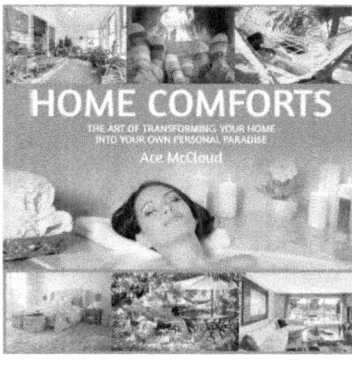

Check out my website at: www.AcesEbooks.com for a complete list of all of my books and high quality audio books. I enjoy bringing you the best knowledge in the world and wish you the best in using this information to make your journey through life better and more enjoyable! **Best of luck to you!**

www.ingramcontent.com/pod-product-compliance
Lightning Source LLC
Chambersburg PA
CBHW051427070526
44584CB00023B/3613